EARTH

ROBERT DAILY

EARTH

FRANKLIN WATTS
A Division of Grolier Publishing
New York London Hong Kong Sydney
Danbury, Connecticut

To Janet

Cover photograph © NASA

Photographs copyright ©: NASA: pp. 8, 26, 31, 43, 47; Culver
Pictures, Inc.: p. 11; Photo Researchers, Inc.: pp. 15 (Julian
Baum/SPL), 18 (Chris Butler/SPL), 23 (Wards Scientific/SS), 37
(Soames Summerhays), 39 (Kees Van Den Berg), 50 (Will and
Deni McIntyre), 52 top (Tim Davis), 52 bottom (Gregory G.
Dimijian), 57 (Dr. Morley Read/SPL); U. S. Geological Survey: pp.
29, 35 (R. E. Wallace); Peter Rosenbaum, 1993: p 64.

Library of Congress Cataloging-in-Publication Data

Daily, Robert
    Earth / by Robert Daily
       p. cm. — (First book)
    Includes bibliographical references and index.
    ISBN 0-531-20158-9 (l.b. bdg.)—ISBN 0-531-15767-9 (pbk.)
    1. Earth—Juvenile literature. Earth] I. Title. II. Series.
QB631.4.D35 1994
525—dc20   93-6102   CIP   AC

FRANKLIN WATTS
A Division of Grolier Publishing
Sherman Turnpike
Danbury, CT 06813

CONTENTS

THE BLUE PLANET

CHAPTER ONE

Zooming through the universe in a spaceship, alien travelers might not be surprised to come across a large pinwheel-shaped *galaxy*. There are billions of such galaxies in the universe. Nor would they be shocked to find a medium-size star on the outskirts of that galaxy. There are billions of stars much larger than this one.

Circling this star are a few relatively tiny spheres floating in space. There is nothing unusual about that. As they get closer, our travelers might notice that one of the spheres is nearly all blue — this is maybe a bit unusual.

A tiny blue speck circling an ordinary star near the edge of one galaxy among billions — that's us. That is Earth.

A photo of Earth taken by the Apollo 17 astronauts as they traveled toward the moon. The south polar ice cap is located on the bottom.

Viewed from a distance, Earth is hardly impressive. But once you get to know it, our speck is a pretty extraordinary place.

That blueness — caused by oceans of water that cover nearly three-fourths of the surface — is one of the things that makes Earth so special. None of the other eight planets in our solar system can boast of liquid water in any amount. These oceans, in turn, make it possible for the single most interesting fact about Earth: It is the only planet we know of that can support life.

Of all the species of life, human beings are the only ones who can explore our planet's past and present, and plan for its future. So let's start exploring Earth, our extraordinary home.

ANCIENT BELIEFS

In ancient times, people were often frightened by Earth's shakes and shudders. So they made up stories to explain what was happening. To tribes in western Africa, Earth was a giant, and an earthquake was simply the giant shaking his head, trying to get the "lice" (people and animals) out of his "hair" (the jungle where they lived). Ancient Japanese people had a different idea about earthquakes. Their theory was that Earth rides on top of a giant catfish. When the fish shook its back, the ground moved.

Other mysteries were explained by equally wonderful stories. To the people of New Zealand, mountains had been pushed out of Earth by a giant fish trying to spit out a hook. To Polynesians, the Hawaiian Islands were left over from a giant battle between the goddess Pele and her sister Namakaokahai. Pele ended up in a Hawaiian volcano, and when she was angry she let everyone know it!

EARLY ASTRONOMERS

Soon the people of Earth were not content with myths. They began looking for other explanations of the planet's movements. Earliest known reports described Earth as a flat sheet at the center of the universe, with the sun, moon, and planets revolving around it. In the sixth century B.C., however, a Greek named Pythagoras noticed that ships seemed to drop below the horizon as they sailed off into the distance. He concluded that Earth was round like a ball (a *sphere*).

An imaginary meeting of three great
astronomers: Aristotle, Ptolemy, and Copernicus.
Copernicus proved that the sun, not the Earth,
was at the center of our planetary system.

Although Pythagoras was perfectly correct, and though later Greek thinkers such as Aristotle (fourth century B.C.) agreed with him, the idea of a round Earth was not completely accepted for nearly two thousand years. When Columbus set sail in 1492, there were still people who thought his ships would drop off the edge of the flat Earth.

In the third century B.C., another Greek named Aristarchus suggested that Earth and the other planets revolved around the sun. Again, this belief was not fully accepted until much later, when Nicolaus Copernicus (1473–1543) proved that the sun, and not Earth, was at the heart of the solar system.

The Greeks had many modern ideas about our planet. About 250 B.C. the Greek astronomer Eratosthenes was able to estimate the circumference of (the distance around) Earth. He observed that when the sun was directly overhead the Egyptian town of Syene, it shone at a 7-degree angle in his city of Alexandria. Knowing this angle, and the distance between the two cities, he was able to calculate a figure that was very close to the correct one.

THE MODERN AGE

By the twentieth century, you might think that we had solved the planet's mysteries. But as late as 1957, scientists still had more questions than answers. They could not adequately explain earthquakes, for example. They had no clue about what went on at the ocean's bottom.

In 1957, though, scientists from sixty countries came together for something called the International Geophysical Year. For more than a year, they studied all aspects of Earth. They measured the atmosphere and magnetic field. They plunged into steaming volcanoes; they dived to the ocean floor. In the years following 1957, they launched space satellites that could send back pictures of the ocean floor.

The years since that International Geophysical Year have brought a revolution in what we know about our planet. Scientists once thought Earth was like a lump of rock — solid and unchanging. Now they know that, like a living body, Earth is constantly changing, moving, and rearranging its parts!

THE BIRTH OF EARTH

CHAPTER TWO

To tell the story of Earth properly, we have to go back farther than 250 B.C. To begin at the very beginning, we have to go back some 5 billion years, give or take a few million — back to an age when our planet was a steaming, red-hot ball of dust and gas.

THE BIG BANG

Around 10 or 20 billion years ago, everything in the universe condensed into one incredibly dense small spot and exploded. Scientists call this the Big Bang. The explosion flung a huge amount of matter into space. Today this cloud of matter, which became stars, galaxies, plan-

An artist's impression of the Big Bang, the colossal explosion that created the universe about 10 or 20 billion years ago.

ets, and everything else in the universe, are still expanding from the force of the Big Bang. This material expanded in every direction and became atoms and then everything else. Among all this, one pinwheel-shaped galaxy is of special interest — our own Milky Way.

About 4.6 billion years ago, on the edge of the Milky Way, another "cloud" of dust and gas was also shrinking. As it grew smaller, its center became very hot, so hot that a star developed. This star became our sun.

Not all the dust and gas was absorbed by the sun. Some remained outside and formed into lumps that circled the sun. At first there were so many lumps that they were always smashing into each other, forming even bigger lumps. Eventually nine major lumps, or planets, were formed. One of these, the third lump from the sun, was Earth.

You wouldn't have recognized our planet during its first billion years. A ball of red-hot rock, it shook from constant earthquakes and volcanic eruptions and was pounded by meteorites and other space "garbage." There was no land or water, no air that humans could breathe. It was definitely not a fit place for man or beast!

After hundreds of millions of years, Earth started to lose some of the heat left over from its formation. Vapor clouds formed and rained water on the surface. The water pooled, forming lakes and oceans. Eventually Earth settled down to be a planet we would recognize.

SHAPE AND SIZE

A few basic facts about Earth have remained the same for billions of years. Like all the planets, ours is a sphere. It is not, however, *perfectly* round. The Earth bulges just slightly at the *equator*, the imaginary line around the middle of the planet, and is slightly flatter at the North and South poles. Scientists call this an *oblate* (slightly flattened) sphere.

The bulge is not too great, however. From pole to pole Earth's *diameter* measures 7,900 miles (12,714 km). Around the equator the diameter is 7,926 miles (12,761 km), making Earth the fifth largest planet in our solar system.

Other measurements have shown that the North Pole is about 80 feet (24.4 m) farther from Earth's center than the South Pole. This means that the Northern *Hemisphere* of the planet is slightly longer than the Southern

The birth of a solar system. In this artist's version, a whirling cloud of dust and gas, which looks like a red disk, condenses to form a sun and planetary system.

Hemisphere, giving Earth an extremely slight pear shape.

ORBIT

It takes 365.244 days, a period of time we call a year, for Earth to orbit the sun. To anyone standing on the surface, our planet seems to be standing still. This is far from the case: as it orbits, Earth races through space at 65,000 miles (105,000 km) per hour. Because the path of this orbit is not exactly round, Earth is slightly closer to the sun in January than in July.

ROTATION

If Earth is closer to the sun in January than in July, then why is January (in the Northern Hemisphere, at least) the colder month? The Earth's axis is not at a right angle to the path of its orbit, but is tilted at a 23.5-degree angle. As Earth orbits the sun, this imaginary axis is always pointing toward the same point in space.

In June, when the Northern Hemisphere is tilted *toward* the sun, it receives the sun's rays more directly; the weather is warmer. In January, the same area is tilted away from the sun; the weather is cooler. It is Earth's tilted axis that gives us our seasons.

It takes Earth 23 hours, 56 minutes, and 4.09 seconds, a period of time we call a day, to make one complete rotation around its axis.

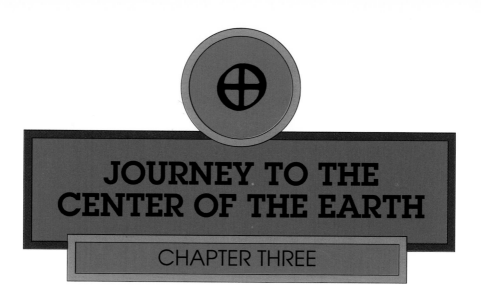

JOURNEY TO THE CENTER OF THE EARTH

CHAPTER THREE

In 1864, a Frenchman named Jules Verne wrote a book called *Journey to the Center of the Earth*. It was a fantasy, but Verne imagined that someday humans would be able to burrow deep into the middle of the planet.

More than a hundred years later, we haven't come much closer to Earth's center than in Verne's day. In fact, the deepest hole ever dug went down about 10 miles (16 km). Reaching the center would take a hole nearly 4,000 miles (6,500 km) deep; we've got a long way to go!

Still, scientists using sophisticated instruments have learned a good deal about the layers of Earth beneath our feet.

THE CORE

Earth has the highest average *density* of all the planets. We know that rocks found on the surface are not especially dense, which means the center of the planet, the core, must be very dense indeed.

The core has two layers. The inner core, the very center, is about 800 miles (1,300 km) thick. It is made mostly of iron, with some nickel, and appears to be solid. The outer core extends another 1,400 miles (2,250 km) from the inner core. It, too, is made of iron and nickel, but, unlike the inner core, it is probably molten (or melted).

THE MANTLE

Wrapped around the core, the *mantle* returns us to solid ground. About 1,800 miles (2,900 km) thick, it starts halfway from the center and extends almost to the surface. The mantle makes up more than 80 percent of Earth's total volume. Though not as dense as the core, the mantle consists of heavy rock containing the metals magnesium and iron. It is solid, unlike the outer core, but hot enough to be slightly soft.

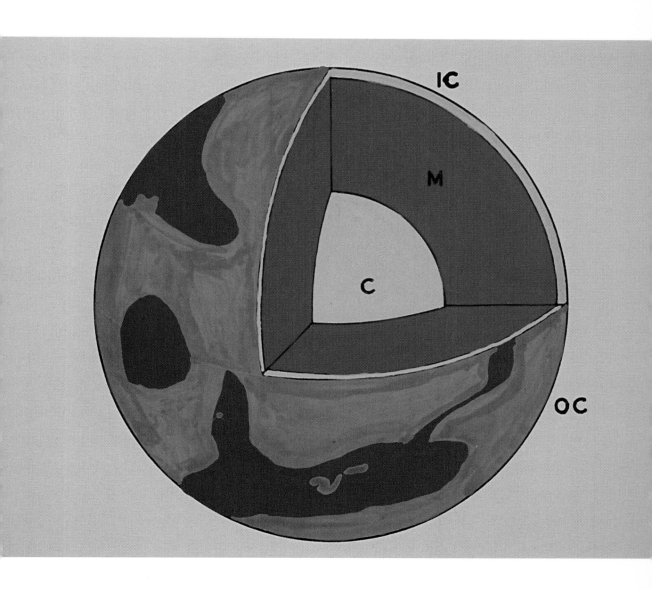

This cross-section of the Earth reveals the layers beneath our feet: the dense core (C), the rocky mantle (M), and the thin inner (IC) and outer (OC) crusts.

THE CRUST

The crust is Earth's skin, and a very thin skin it is, only 20 to 40 miles (32 to 64 km) thick under the continents. Beneath the oceans it is even thinner, extending between 3 and 20 miles (5 and 32 km).

Because it's so close to us, the crust is the layer we know the most about. It is made up of rock, called bedrock, which is solid. Yet the crust is very unstable, broken into a dozen or so *plates*, which are floating on top of the mantle. These plates are restless, sometimes pulling apart, sometimes crashing head-on.

TEMPERATURES

The tremendous heat at Earth's center prevents a real-life journey. Scientists figure that the temperature increases about 85° F (30° C) for every mile (1.6 km) you go down. The temperature of the mantle ranges from between 8,000° F (4,400° C) to 11,000° F (6,000° C). The core can be as hot as 13,000° F (7,100° C).

Where does all this heat come from? Some of it is left over from Earth's fiery birth; rocks are able to retain heat for a very long time, even 5 billion years. The rest is actually created by rocks in the interior. These rocks contain radioactive elements, such as uranium and thorium, that produce heat by emitting particles and rays.

GRAVITY

Gravity is the invisible force that pulls objects toward a planet. It keeps a pole vaulter from soaring off into space or a thrown baseball from traveling to the moon. It also keeps the moon orbiting around Earth, and Earth moving around the sun.

The farther you travel from Earth's center, the less gravitational pull you'll feel; gravity is stronger at sea level than, say, on top of Mount Everest. Even at the same level, the effect of gravity changes. Its pull is slightly greater when you're standing on a heavy, dense rock than when you're on a light rock.

Earth is also affected by the gravity of its nearest neighbor, the moon. The pull of the moon's gravity causes our oceans to rise and fall. We call these movements *tides*.

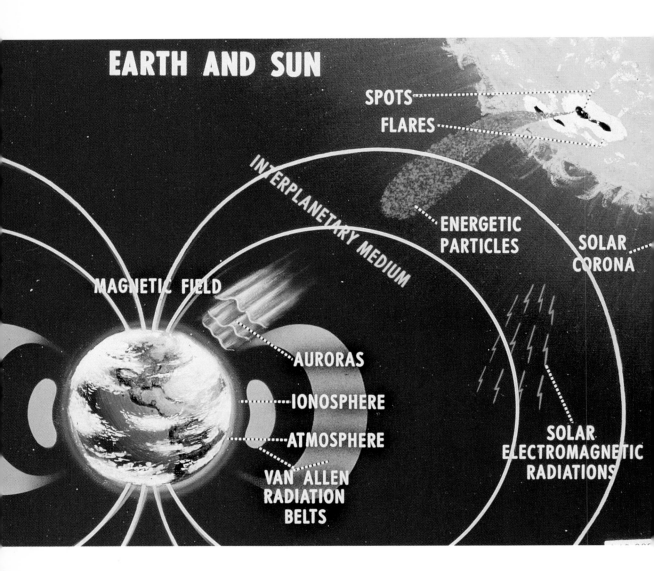

EARTH AND SUN

SPOTS
FLARES

INTERPLANETARY MEDIUM

ENERGETIC PARTICLES

SOLAR CORONA

MAGNETIC FIELD

AURORAS

IONOSPHERE

ATMOSPHERE

SOLAR ELECTROMAGNETIC RADIATIONS

VAN ALLEN RADIATION BELTS

Earth has a magnetic field, which is caused by molten metals spinning at the planet's core. The sun also sends off electromagnetic radiations.

THE MAGNETIC FIELD

At most locations on Earth, a bar magnet will always point approximately north. Earth itself is like a huge magnet. The ends of this magnet are near the North and South poles. Surrounding Earth is a *magnetic field*, an unseen area where the magnetic force extends.

Where does Earth's magnetic field come from? Scientists think the answer lies at the planet's center. Remember that the outer core is made up of melted iron and nickel. These liquid metals (according to the theory) spin around the solid-metal inner core. As they move, they set up an electrical current, turning the core into a giant magnet.

OUR RESTLESS EARTH

CHAPTER FOUR

The planet Earth is made up of four basic elements: earth, water, air, and living beings. These have been named with Greek words: *lithosphere* (from *lithos*, or stone), *hydrosphere* (*hydros*, water), *atmosphere* (*atmos*, vapor), and *biosphere* (*bios*, life). In this chapter we examine the lithosphere, the surface we walk and drive and build houses on.

People sometimes talk about "standing on solid ground." In the past couple of decades, though, scientists have learned that the ground we stand on is anything *but* solid. In fact, Earth's crust is cracked like an eggshell, and the pieces are constantly on the move — lifting, dropping, shaking, quaking, and colliding with themselves!

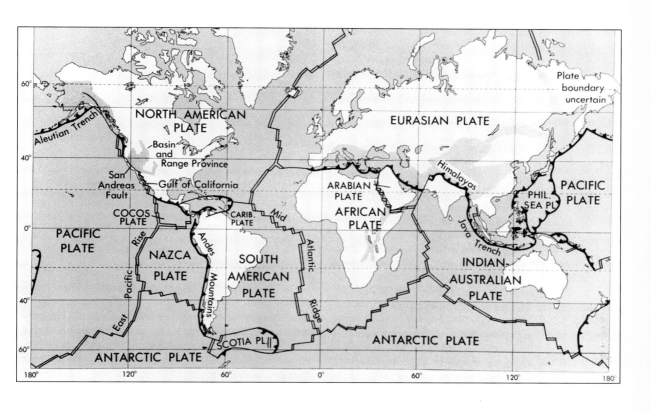

60°

NORTH AMERICAN PLATE

Aleutian Trench

Basin and Range Province

San Andreas Fault

Gulf of California

COCOS PLATE

PACIFIC PLATE

NAZCA PLATE

Pacific Rise

East

40°

EURASIAN PLATE

Plate boundary uncertain

ARABIAN PLATE

AFRICAN PLATE

Himalayas

PACIFIC PLATE

PHIL. SEA PL.

0°

CARIB. PLATE

Mid

Andes Mountains

SOUTH AMERICAN PLATE

Atlantic

Ridge

Java Trench

INDIAN-AUSTRALIAN PLATE

40°

SCOTIA PL.

ANTARCTIC PLATE

ANTARCTIC PLATE

60°

180°   120°   60°   0°   60°   120°   180°

This map shows the plates that make up
Earth's crust. The North American and
Pacific plates meet at the famous San
Andreas Fault, which runs along the
coast of California.

29

PLATE TECTONICS

The dozen or so plates that make up Earth's crust are enormous, each covering millions of square miles. Between 40 and 50 miles (64 and 80 km) thick, each is made of a layer of crust on a slab of solid mantle.

These plates are always slowly moving. We can't see or feel them move because they travel only an inch or two (2.5 to 5 cm) every year. Like huge rafts, they are floating on the soft layer of mantle beneath the solid mantle. Their "passengers" are the oceans and the seven *continents*: North and South America, Europe, Asia, Africa, Australia, and Antarctica.

The science of studying these movements is called *plate tectonics*, from the Greek *tekton*, to build.

A PLACE CALLED PANGAEA

Movement of only an inch or two (2.5 to 5 cm) every year may not sound like much. But over the billions of years Earth has existed, it has added up to a lot of movement. Scientists believe that about 200 million years ago, the continents were all clumped together into one "supercontinent." They call this huge landmass

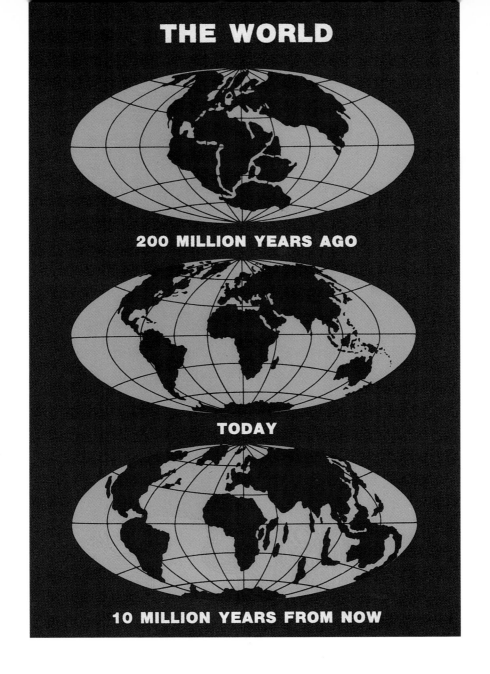

THE WORLD

200 MILLION YEARS AGO

TODAY

10 MILLION YEARS FROM NOW

About 200 million years ago, the continents were clumped together in one giant mass (above). Today that landmass has split into the seven continents (middle); in 10 million years they will spread even farther apart (bottom).

Pangaea (pan-GEE-ah), meaning "all Earth." This supercontinent began to break up about the time dinosaurs started roaming Earth.

How do scientists know the continents started in one big clump? As is often the case, there is no exact proof. But there are many clues pointing in this direction. The first clue is quite simple. Look at a map of Earth. Certain continents fit together like pieces of a giant jigsaw puzzle! For example, the west coast of Africa seems to fit against the east coast of South America.

Other clues are found in the crust. Rocks found on opposite sides of the Atlantic — in Africa and in Brazil, for example, and in Scotland and in Labrador — are almost identical. And plant *fossils*, found in both South America and Africa, also match up. The development of such similar rocks and plants is too much to be called coincidence. At some point, the continents must have been pushed together.

So scientists are quite sure that the plates are pulling apart (a theory they call "continental drift"). But this raises another question: What makes the plates and continents so restless? This time the answer is found underwater. In the middle of the Atlantic Ocean is a giant crack, 7 to 30 miles (11 to 48 km) wide and nearly a mile (1.6 km) deep, between two plates. Scientists think that *magma* is forced up through this crack. When the magma cools, it turns into rock and becomes part of the plates on either side of the crack. The plates are pushed apart, about one inch (2.5 cm) every year.

CLIMB EVERY MOUNTAIN

As we said, tectonics means building. And plate tectonics has built much of Earth's landscape. Mountains are formed when two plates collide head-on. The force causes the plates to crumple and push up into soaring peaks. The Himalaya mountains, for example, were built when the Indian plate pushed against the Eurasian plate.

Geologists were surprised to find fossils of ancient sea creatures high up in the Himalayas. They now believe there was once an ocean between the two plates that created the Himalayas. This ocean floor was pushed thousands of feet into the air when the plates collided.

WHOLE LOT OF SHAKING

When plates meet, they also can rub together for a long time. Then, all of a sudden, one plate breaks free and jerks forward a few feet. We call this an earthquake.

Most quakes occur on a *fault*. One of the most famous is the San Andreas Fault, which splits the west coast of North America. The Pacific plate, carrying part of California on its back, is slowly traveling north, separating from the North American plate. In 15 million years, Los Angeles will practically be a neighbor of San Francisco!

There have been nearly forty major earthquakes along the San Andreas Fault in the past 150 years. In 1906, the San Francisco quake left 503 people dead and caused $350 million in damages. During that tremor, a redwood tree that straddles the fault near San Francisco was split in half. A piece of the trunk was dragged nearly 8 feet (2.44 m). The tree stands today as a monument to Earth's destructive power. California continues to have frequent quakes, even if not as strong as the one in 1906.

Earthquakes also affect the hydrosphere, creating huge tidal waves, or tsunamis. A typi-

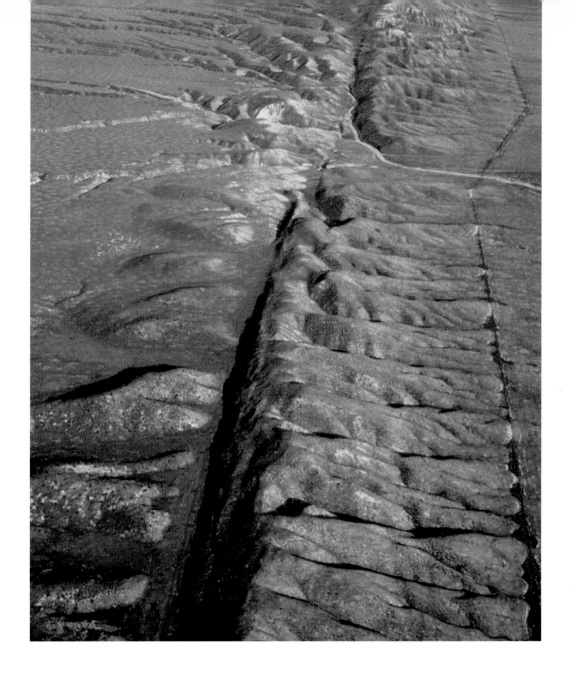

The San Andreas Fault, seen near San Luis Obispo, California. There have been nearly forty major earthquakes along this fault in the past 150 years, including a deadly one in 1906.

cal tsunami is 90 miles (145 km) long and travels at 450 miles (724 km) per hour.

FIERY VOLCANOES

Plates don't always collide or rub together. Sometimes, one plate slides under the other and is pushed toward the center of Earth. (This is called *subduction*.) When it gets deep enough, it melts and becomes magma. Eventually some of this magma emerges through a crack or opening in Earth's crust. This is called a volcano.

Like earthquakes, most volcanoes are found on the edges of plates. The biggest stretch of volcanoes, called the Ring of Fire, forms a circle around the Pacific Ocean, from California across to Japan.

Some volcanoes are fairly quiet. At other times the magma, called *lava* when it reaches the surface, bursts through in a spectacular explosion of gas, steam, and rock. The lava, at temperatures of between 1,000° and 2,000° F (approximately 550° and 1,100° C), can have great destructive power.

Volcanoes don't just destroy; they also create. In April 1973, there were several eruptions

This fiery volcano erupted in Hawaii in 1983. A line of active volcanoes called the Ring of Fire passes through Hawaii as it stretches from California to Japan.

off the coast of Japan. Within five months, enough lava had risen above sea level to create a new island, called Nishimo. Scientists believe that most of Japan was formed in exactly this way during the past 30 million years.

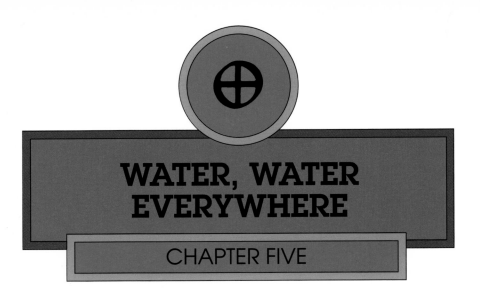

WATER, WATER EVERYWHERE

CHAPTER FIVE

Although we call it Planet Earth, a better name might be Planet Ocean! Nearly three-fourths of Earth's surface is covered with water. The Pacific Ocean alone takes up about one-third of the planet. It's larger in area than all land put together.

No other planet in the solar system has this huge system of oceans. It's one of the things that makes Earth special — and keeps us alive. The oceans feed us. They determine our weather and climate. And scientists believe the oceans are where life began billions of years ago. In other words, the oceans are essential to life. Yet until a few decades ago this huge area was unknown territory. Even today we have much to learn.

There's more water on Earth's surface than anything else. This picture of the Atlantic Ocean was taken off the coast of France.

PULLING THE PLUG

Earth has seven major oceans: North and South Atlantic, North and South Pacific, Indian, Arctic, and Antarctic. Along with lakes, rivers, and gulfs, they cover about 140 million square miles (360 million sq km). The oceans have an average depth of between 2.5 and 7 miles (4 and 11 km).

What would our planet look like if we could pull the plug and let all the water run out? Until recently, people thought the ocean floor was perfectly flat. Now we know that the exact opposite is true. The bottom of the ocean is a rugged landscape of volcanoes, trenches, and ridges — including the longest mountain range on the planet! Wrapped around Earth like seams on a giant baseball, this range stretches for 47,000 miles (75,700 km). In the middle of the Atlantic Ocean it reaches as high as 11,700 feet (3,570 km). Sometimes, like a giant sea serpent coming up for air, the ridge pokes its back above the surface, creating islands.

The ocean basin is also broken up by a series of deep cracks, called trenches. The deepest trench yet discovered, found in the Pacific Ocean near Guam, is more than 36,198 feet (11,040 m) deep.

OCEANS ON THE MOVE

Oceans are constantly on the move. In seas near the North and South poles, water at the surface is chilled, and therefore heavier. It slowly sinks to the bottom, where it forces warmer (and lighter) water to the surface. The trip from top to bottom and back again can take more than a thousand years.

Waves are another source of movement. They are caused by wind.

Currents are caused by Earth's rotation. They work under the surface, like "rivers" within the ocean, traveling in many directions at various speeds. Currents help to control our weather, by carrying warm or cold climates from one area to another. England, for example, has warmer weather than Labrador, even though they are equally far north, because a current called the Gulf Stream carries warm water from the Gulf of Mexico to England's shores.

Finally, water is constantly moving *out* of the oceans. The water evaporates, or turns into vapor, moving from the ocean to the atmosphere. This warm vapor rises to higher and colder levels. When it becomes cold enough, it condenses, or turns into water droplets — rain, sleet, snow — and falls back to Earth, refilling the oceans and supplying the land with vital water. This process is called the water cycle.

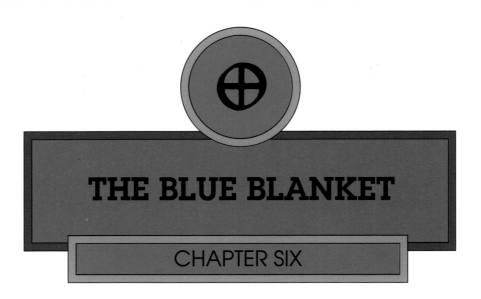

THE BLUE BLANKET

CHAPTER SIX

From the surface of Earth, the atmosphere appears to be a blue blanket of air wrapped around the planet. We may live *on* Earth, but we live *in* the atmosphere. The atmosphere is actually invisible, so we sometimes take it for granted. But where would we be without it? The atmosphere lets us breathe the oxygen we need to survive. It protects us from the sun's harmful rays, and from flying objects from space that would otherwise come crashing down to the ground. And it maintains an even temperature, so we don't burn up during the day or freeze during the night.

It is obvious from this photograph why Earth is known as "the blue planet." In the entire universe it's the only planet we know of that supports life.

RECIPE FOR LIFE

The atmosphere of Earth is much thicker than those of Mars or Mercury, though it's pretty thin compared to those of Jupiter, Saturn, or Venus. Gravity is the key. It is Earth's gravity that holds the gas *molecules* and keeps them from drifting into space. Mercury doesn't have a strong enough gravitational pull to hold on to any but the thinnest atmosphere.

The most common ingredient in our atmosphere is nitrogen. It makes up 78 percent (by volume) of the air. Nearly 21 percent consists of oxygen molecules. The remaining 1 percent is made up of a variety of gases — argon, carbon dioxide, neon, helium, krypton, hydrogen, xenon, and nitrous oxide.

This mixture of invisible gases creates a perfect balance for life. It has, for example, just the right amount of oxygen. With less oxygen, living creatures could not breathe. But if the atmosphere had a little more oxygen, such as 25 percent instead of 21 percent, much of what's on Earth, including houses and forests, could burst into flames!

Even the minor ingredients contribute to the balance. For example: carbon dioxide makes up only .03 percent of the atmosphere but is essential to life. It lets the sun's rays through to heat Earth, but doesn't allow heat waves to escape. Too much carbon dioxide would trap so much warmth that our planet would over-heat. By this process (commonly known as the greenhouse effect), we maintain an ideal tem-perature.

LAYERS OF AIR

Earth's "ocean of air" is much deeper than any of its saltwater oceans. Starting at the surface, it extends upward more than 1,000 miles (1,600 km)! (The Sears Tower in Chicago, the world's tallest building, is less than half a mile high.) Not until we reach this faraway point does Earth officially end and outer space begin. But Earth's atmosphere doesn't end sud-denly. It gets thinner and thinner the higher we go, until it thins out into the vacuum of outer space.

Scientists divide the atmosphere into five layers. The first 10 miles (16 km) are called the *troposphere*, after the Greek word for "turning." And the troposphere is, in fact, constantly turning. It is here that we find storms, thunder, lightning — the happenings we call weather.

The next layer, the *stratosphere*, extends 30 miles (48 km) from the surface. Airplane pilots like to fly here because they don't have to worry about the winds and storms of the troposphere. In fact, when you fly in a long-distance jet, you're pretty much flying at the base of the stratosphere. You'll notice most of the clouds are beneath you and that the sky above is almost clear blue.

The *mesosphere* extends another 50 miles (80 km). It is here that the atmosphere reaches its lowest temperature, about $-135°$ F ($-93°$ C).

The layer from 50 to 300 miles (80 to 480 km) above Earth's surface is the *ionosphere*. It is made up of ions, molecules that have been electrically charged by the sun's radiation.

The *exosphere* is the very thin final layer, extending more than 1,000 miles (1,600 km) above Earth's surface.

The weight of the gases pulled by gravity toward Earth is known as *air pressure*. Like gravity, air pressure becomes lower as you travel higher. The thickest layer is at the surface, because the weight of the air above squeezes the gas molecules together. In fact, 99 percent of the atmosphere's mass is packed into the bottom 50 miles (80 km).

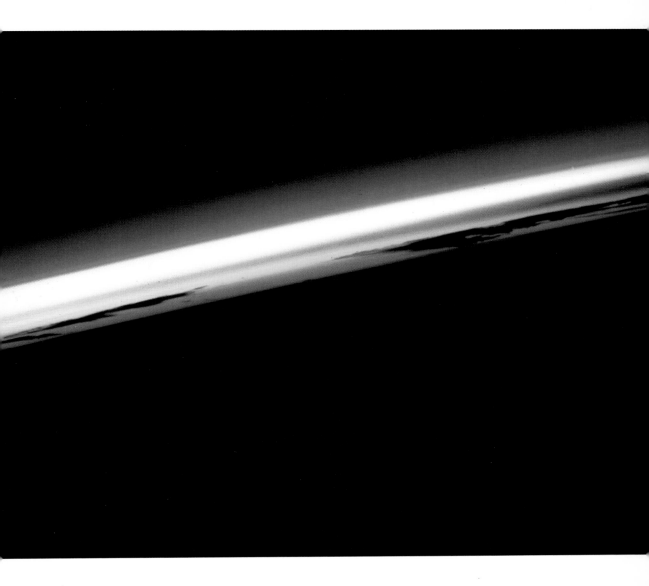

The layers of Earth's atmosphere are evident in this photo shot from a satellite at an altitude of 128 miles. Below the stratosphere, the lower atmosphere appears dark red because of dust and smoke from a recent volcano eruption.

THE RESTLESS WIND

Like Earth's oceans and crust, the atmosphere is very restless, constantly changing and churning. Light from the sun heats Earth, warming the air closest to the surface. The warm, light air rises while cool, heavy air sinks to take its place.

Air is also moving along the surface as the atmosphere constantly warms the equatorial regions much more than polar areas. Hot air at the equator rises; cold air from the North and South poles flows toward the equator in the form of wind to take its place.

At a higher altitude, the warm air returns from the equator toward the poles. Earth's turning motion also affects wind directions in an east-to-west manner.

Even the gas molecules that make up the atmosphere are always changing. One example: Animals breathe in oxygen, and breathe out carbon dioxide. While this is happening, plants are doing the exact opposite — removing carbon dioxide, and releasing oxygen. Just by breathing, we help to maintain the perfect balance!

LIFE ON EARTH

CHAPTER SEVEN

Finally we come to the part of Earth that includes *us* — the biosphere. But not *just* us. Earth holds millions of forms of life, more than can be counted. Some, like bacteria, are invisible without a microscope. Others, like whales or sequoia trees, are so huge they dwarf human beings. But all life-forms have one thing in common — in all of the universe Earth is the only planet we know of that supports life.

BUILDING BLOCKS OF LIFE

The biosphere is the area where plants and animals can live. Compared to Earth as a

Rain forests, such as this one in Costa Rica, are home to half of all plant and animal species in the world. It is estimated that as we destroy the forests, we lose one species every day.

whole, the biosphere is a tiny sliver, extending into only the lowest levels of the atmosphere, and only a few dozen feet into the soil. (The ocean is an exception; it is teeming with life at all levels.)

The biosphere cannot exist without the other three spheres; they work together to make Earth a good place for life. Water, for example, is essential to every living being. The soil provides nutrients for plants and other creatures. Oxygen, too, is needed by almost every creature.

And life could not exist without the sun. All food comes from the sun either directly — if we eat fruit or vegetables — or indirectly — if we eat meat from animals that have eaten fruit or vegetables. The sun keeps us at just the right temperature — too hot and our water would evaporate, too cold and it would freeze over.

ALL CREATURES GREAT AND SMALL

There is a tremendous variety of life on Earth. Some scientists think there are as many as 10 million species of plants and animals. However, only 1.4 million species have been found and named. More than half of these

The scarlet macaw (above) and white-faced capuchins (below) are among the many animals endangered by the destruction of the rain forest. Both species are native to Costa Rica.

species are insects. Birds make up 9,000 species; mammals, only 4,000.

Some species are found all over the globe. Human beings, for example, have practically taken over — there are more than 5 billion of us. Other species live in very small areas. In the tropics near the equator, for example, some species are found only in a single valley, or on one tiny island.

THE BEGINNING OF LIFE

The planet Earth existed at least a billion years before life made its first appearance. (The oldest fossil ever found is about 3.5 billion years old.)

How did life begin? In 1953 a college graduate student named Stanley Miller tried to answer that question by re-creating conditions for early life in a bottle. Actually, he gathered the gases that were present when Earth was young — methane, ammonia, hydrogen, water vapor. He heated these gases (Earth was very hot in its early stages), and for good measure sent sparks shooting through the bottle to represent lightning. After one week, he found he had "created" several kinds of molecules called *amino acids.*

These amino acids, scientists think, were the building blocks of life. They bonded together to create complex bigger molecules called proteins. And the proteins combined to form even more complicated creatures that could reproduce. Very, very slowly, these creatures became life as we know it.

We *Homo sapiens* (the name given to our species) are truly late arrivers. It's impossible to say exactly when the earliest humans appeared, but many scientists think it happened between 4 and 6 million years ago. If the life span of Earth were equal to one day, then human beings would have appeared only in the last several minutes!

THE FUTURE OF THE EARTH

We've been talking about Earth's perfect balance — how the conditions on Earth are just right for life, and for human life in particular.

Unfortunately, humans are not always as good to Earth as Earth is to humans. That "perfect balance" is very delicate. As Homo sapiens grow in numbers, and spread out searching for food and fuel, we are in danger of throwing the balance off.

We are, for example, fouling the atmosphere with our industrial and motor vehicle waste. Every year, we send more than 300 million tons of pollutants into the air. Rain full of these pollutants is falling on our soil and gathering in our lakes and oceans.

By burning fuels such as coal and oil, we send more and more carbon dioxide into the atmosphere. As we noted earlier, too much carbon dioxide traps heat at the Earth's surface. Scientists fear that average temperatures could rise 3.6° F (2 °C) by the year 2040. Someday, if temperatures continue to rise, the ice caps at the North and South poles could melt, which would raise the sea level and flood hundreds of coastal cities such as New York City (among innumerable others).

Plants, especially trees, can help absorb carbon dioxide. But we are busy chopping them down. In the past ten years, we have destroyed half a billion acres of the world's tropical rain forests, at a rate of 30 acres (12.14 hectares) per minute, twenty-four hours a day! These forests house half of all plant and animal species in the world. Scientists estimate that, as we gobble up the forests, we may be losing one species every day.

So the future of Earth does not look good at present. Fortunately, though, it is not too late to improve the situation. In recent years, we have learned that humans can change our planet for *good* as well as ill. Alone among all Earth's creatures, we can control the fate of our planet.

How much longer can Earth survive this kind of destruction? These trees in Ecuador — the heart of the Amazon rain forest — have been burned down to make room for a new village.

In 1992, some 30,000 people — including 100 world leaders — met in Brazil for an Earth Summit. They talked about the rain-forest destruction, about pollution, about the carbon dioxide dilemma. Though none of these problems can be solved by one meeting, the summit shows that the people of Earth are concerned about the kind of planet that you — and your children, and their children — will inherit.

Earth has lasted some 4.6 billion years. If we take good care of it, it's bound to last a few billion more.

FACT SHEET ON EARTH

Symbol for Earth — ⊕

Position — Earth is the third planet from the sun, positioned between Venus and Mars.

Rotation period — 23 hours, 56 minutes, 4.09 seconds.

Length of year — 365.244 days.

Diameter — 7,926 miles (12,760 km) at equator; 7,900 miles (12,719 km) at the poles.

Average distance from the sun — 92,956,000 miles (149,659,000 km).

Total surface area — 197,000,000 square miles (510,000,000 square km).

Highest point — Mount Everest: 29,028 feet (8,853 m).

Lowest point — Marianas Trench: 36,198 feet (11,040 m).

Number of moons — Earth has only one moon, located an average distance of 238,857 miles (384,560 km) from the Earth's center. It is 2,160 miles (3,478 km) in diameter.

GLOSSARY

Amino acids — one of the building blocks from which plants and animals are made

Atmosphere — the various gases that surround a planet

Axis — the imaginary line through a planet's center, around which it rotates

Biosphere — the area on Earth where plants and animals can live

Continents — the seven major bodies of land that make up Earth's surface

Core — the innermost part of a planet

Crust — the rocky, outermost layer of a planet

Density — the compactness of materials

Diameter — the distance across a circle or sphere

Equator — the imaginary line that circles Earth halfway between the poles

Fault — a crack in Earth's crust where two plates meet

Fossil — an impression in rock of an ancient plant or animal that has been preserved in Earth's crust

Galaxy — an enormous assemblage of stars, planets, gas, and dust. Earth is located in the Milky Way Galaxy

Gravity — an unseen force that pulls objects toward a planet's center and keeps planets, moons, and spacecraft around a larger body

Greenhouse effect — term used to describe what happens when carbon dioxide traps heat in Earth's atmosphere

Hemisphere — either the northern or southern half of Earth, as divided by the equator

Homo sapiens — the scientific name for human beings

Hydrosphere — the waters of Earth

Lava — molten rock (or magma) after it issues from a volcano

Lithosphere — the rocky crust of Earth

Magma — molten rock under Earth's crust

Magnetic field — the area around a planet that causes a compass needle to point to the magnetic poles

Mantle — the rocky middle layer of a planet, between core and crust

Molecule — a small particle of matter, some simple and some very complex, made up of atoms, the smallest building blocks of matter as we know it

Orbit — the curved path of an object circling another object

Oxygen — the gas in Earth's atmosphere that makes life possible

Pangaea — the huge landmass that made up Earth's surface many millions of years ago, before it broke into continents

Plates — sections of Earth's crust that float on the soft mantle. (The science of studying their movement is called plate tectonics.)

FOR FURTHER READING

Ballard, Robert D. *Exploring Our Living Planet.* Washington, D.C.: National Geographic Society, 1983.

Bramwell, Martyn. *Mountains.* New York: Franklin Watts, 1986.

Chapman, Clark R. *The Inner Planets.* New York: Charles Scribner's Sons, 1977.

Gallant, Roy A. *Our Restless Earth.* New York: Franklin Watts, 1986.

Malin, Stuart. *The Greenwich Guide to the Planets.* Cambridge: Cambridge University Press, 1989.

Newton, David. *Earthquakes.* New York: Franklin Watts, 1993.

Vogt, Gregory. *Volcanoes.* New York: Franklin Watts, 1993.

Weiner, Jonathan. *Planet Earth.* New York: Bantam Books, 1986.

INDEX

ABOUT THE AUTHOR

Robert Daily received a B.A. in English literature from Carleton College and a master's degree in English literature from the University of Chicago. He is a magazine writer for both adults and children and is also the author of *Mercury* in the First Book series. He lives with his wife, Janet, in Chicago.